"Journey of The Heart" Series

Vol. 3

"Voyage of the Heart"

Clem Stack Publications Ltd.

## **POEMS**

Poems are groups, of words,
brought to life,
by thoughts,
pen,
and ink.
Like the dew
of a thought,
the ink produces,
its magic
of combined words,
that can make,
you,
perhaps millions,
think.

*Clement Stack*
28/11/2004

**Clem Stack Publications Ltd.**

15, Flower Hill,
Rushbrooke Manor,
Cobh,
Co. Cork,
Ireland.

Tel. No. 021- 4812051
Email: clemstack@eircom.net

A copy of this book can be obtained from:

Trinity College, Dublin
The Universities of Oxford and Cambridge
The National Library of Scotland
The National Library of Wales

All rights reserved, please, no part of this publication may be reproduced, stored in a retrieval system, or transmitted in any form or by any means, electronic, mechanical, photocopying, recording, or otherwise, without the prior written permission of the publisher.
Permission is not nessecery for private use.

*These poems are dedicated to the "broken heart"*

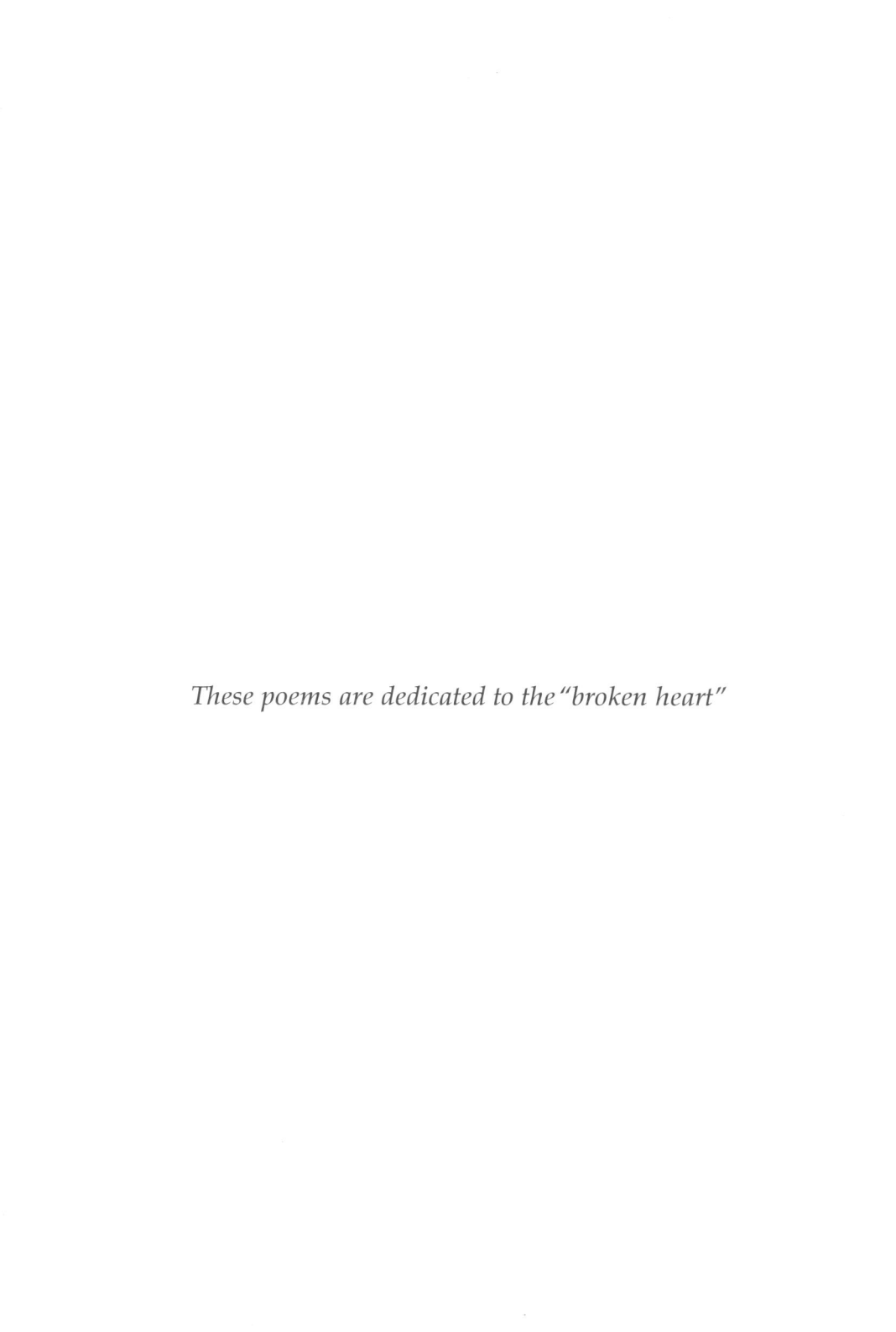

INDEX

1) VOYAGE OF THE HEART ................................................. 2
2) SOMEONE ............................................................................ 3
3) OVER AND OUT ................................................................. 4
4) NO RESCUE REQUIRED ................................................... 6
5) SPEAK TO ME ..................................................................... 7
6) NO AWARENESS ................................................................ 8
7) RIVER BLIND ...................................................................... 9
8) LAST PORT OF CALL ......................................................10
9) IT AIN'T YOU ....................................................................11
10) LOVE LINE .........................................................................12
11) TODAY IS... ........................................................................13
12) DEAR FRIEND ...................................................................14
13) NO SEASONS IN MY HEART ........................................16
14) THE STARE ........................................................................18

## VOYAGE OF THE HEART

It was a voyage of the heart,
It was a voyage of the heart,
dismantling now on the rocks of destiny,
log book stored in the memory of the mind,
ending the voyage of the heart.

The heart, expressed a thank you,
for now the time is right,
it's time to open the curtains,
to the inflow of the light.

Time will become the healer,
the victims the healees,
planning solo journeys
alone to sail life's seas.

It was a voyage of the heart,
It was a voyage of the heart,
dismantling now on the rocks of destiny,
log book stored in the memory of the mind,
ending the voyage of the heart.

One tree does not constitute a forest,
one pebble is not a beach,
at the end of this love's journey,
a conclusion will be reached.

Resting the oars in the oarlocks,
breathing a sigh of relief,
the lifeboat beached her head,
on the peaceful nirvanic shore.

While resting the head in the hands,
gazing at the sands of time,
the waters gently rushed the beach head,
to the melody of a rhyme.

It was a voyage of the heart,
It was a voyage of the heart,
journey over,
log book stored,
ending the journey of the heart.

## SOMEONE

Someone,
      sat on the bank of a river.
Someone,
      smiled a smile of relief.
someone,
      smiled a smile of laughter,
      or was it a smile of grief.

The river,
      softly whispered her message,
      if you don't let it go,
      it can't flow,
      don't interfere with her journey,
      if you love her, let her go.

as the breeze,
      seconded her message,
      the reeds, voted, by taking a bow.
      For cosmic forces were at play,
      in the season of the now.

And someone,
      went into the dream state,
      to be shown what was in store.
      A vision so delightful,
      surprises by the score.

The return,
      of the loved ones,
      identities not to be revealed,
      seizing the opportunities,
      and someone's lips were sealed.

And someone,
      strolled away from the river,
      giving thanks with a smile,
      onwards, with the spiritual journey,
      greeting, the upcoming mile.

## OVER AND OUT

**Coastguard:** Coastguard calling the Relation-Ship.
Are you receiving?
Over.

**Relation-Ship:** Loud and Clear.
Over

**Coastguard:** Do you require assistance?
Over.

**Relation-Ship:** No assistance required, thank you.
Over.

**Coastguard:** Can you declare your intentions please?
Over.

**Relation-Ship:** We are sinking the Relation-Ship.
It is in the best interests of the owners, and has been agreed by all concerned.
Over.

**Coastguard:** We are concerned for you.
Over.

**Relation-Ship:** Everything is fine. The emotional sea is not making the job easy and good memories cannot turn the tide.
Over.

**Coastguard:** Is there any assistance that we can render?
Over.

**Relation-Ship:** A few prayers would help if you have the time.
All is well.
Over

**Coastguard:** Be advised, Relation-Ship.
You are dangerously close to the rocks.
Over.

**Relation-Ship:** Be advised Coastguard, we are proceeding to the Lifeboat Stations.
The two first mates will abandon independently.
Port and starboard sides respectively.
Please notify all shipping in the area.
Over.

**Coastguard:** We are observing your departure.
Over.

**Relation-Ship:** Coastguard, please note Lifeboats are in the water.
*(May God forgive us).*
Over.

**Coastguard:** Gods speed to safety.
Over and out.

**Coastguard:** Attention all shipping in the area.
Be advised.
The Relation-Ship has sunk on the rocks of destiny.
all hands are safe and well, and proceeding to the shoreline.
No assistance required.
Over and out.

## NO RESCUE REQUIRED

Smiling they entered the lifeboats,
for they were leaving the sinking ship,
no S.O.S. for the coastguard,
let it sink, this relation-ship.

The clouds of memories gathered,
growing a smile, on their sinking face,
let it go down to the bottom,
for this sinking is no disgrace.

The sea gulls gathered in their thousands,
flying over the sinking relation-ship,
aware of the out of body observers,
singing, hold on to the friendship.

Together, they smuggled prayers into heaven,
and booze across the state line,
letting family members believe,
that their relation-ship was fine.

They crossed swords on many issues,
ending dialogue, with a hug and a kiss,
experiencing, no real fortunes,
what they never had, they would never miss.

The sea gulls gathered in their thousands,
flying over the sinking relation-ship,
aware of the out of body observers,
singing, hold on to the friendship.

As once, they drifted close together,
now they were drifting apart,
no real plans for the outcome,
as they observed the sea gull choir.

The sea gulls gathered in their thousands,
flying over the sinking relation-ship,
quite aware of the out of body observers,
singing, hold on to the friendship.

## SPEAK TO ME

Speak to me
in words that are soft in tone,
regardless of the subject matter,
in a soft voice, steady and controlled.

Speak to me
in a loving nature,
as if they would be our last words,
for I am receptive to every word.

Speak to me
wearing your smile,
I will listen to your distance,
and understand your extra mile.

Speak to me
with your smiling eyes,
bridled tongue,
and I will smile back.

Speak to me
with your guided silence,
for indeed a loving thought,
is stronger, than any word.

## NO AWARENESS

Out came the news,
unsolicited were their views,
no prepared, plan of attack,
just prepare the victim,
for the family rack.

In the heat of their chase,
forgetting all love and grace,
septic tongues on the attack,
gathered now, to form the pack.

Would the victim scare and run?
Or laugh at them and experience the fun?
The sleeping beauties, with their unbridled tongues,
smell the blood, in the name of "family hood".

## **RIVER BLIND**

Lets turn off the water,
that energises the waterfall of tears,
wishful thinking has its outcome,
waste not, the friendship of years.

For this separating river,
through our lifetime,
it will flow,
what's the point in damning it?
for what's needed, is control of flow.

For the river gives the answer,
as it flows, between you and me,
the river is the middle way,
and some day you will see.

## LAST PORT OF CALL

She offered him no ferry,
and he offered her no bridge,
one viewed it from the valley,
the other, from the ridge.
And their tears of frustration,
rolled down from their cheeks,
time out for the lovers,
a new life, they must seek.

A glancing smile, drew them together,
past lifetimes attracted the crew,
they dared the unchartered waters,
always seeking a new view.
Now, it's their last port of call,
for their voyage, has come to an end,
pleasantries are exchanged,
promised postcards, to be sent.

For the storms, worn out the rigging,
the relation-ship destined for the breakers
yard,
disembarking on the gangway,
in their tears they got jarred.
But in the dockyard of the universe,
spawn the plans for a new ship,
will it be a solo voyage,
or a refitted, crewed-ship?

## IT AIN'T YOU

It ain't you,
because it's definitely me,
and I know you resent it,
but it's the way it's got to be.
Promises should last forever,
but everything runs its course,
and it ain't you,
because it's definitely me.

I never ran out of things to say,
for that would be so sad,
but forcing the words of conversation,
comes, no more easily.
It's not necessary to express in words,
love's feelings to every degree,
and it ain't you,
because it's definitely me.

It ain't you,
because it's definitely me,
angry words rolling off my tongue,
well, soul me, it doesn't agree.
In the silence of divine silence,
is something, that is good for me,
and it ain't you,
because it's definitely me.

It ain't you,
because it's definitely me,
so course, are other vibrations,
from their auras I do flee.
My close contact with the God forces,
brought about the change in me,
and it ain't you,
because it's definitely me.

## LOVE LINE

I offer you a friendship,
not chiselled out of stone,
I offer you a lifetime,
of not travelling alone.
I offer you a love divine,
neither chained, nor tied with twine,
I offer you this offer,
reach out and grab the line.
I offer you jars of certainty,
to be opened, at your will,
I offer you bars of clarity,
when your heart is still.
I offer you bottles of devotion,
to drink when your lips are dry.
I offer you boxes of reality
but not tied up with twine,
I offer you this offer,
reach out and grab the line.

## TODAY IS...

Deep in the night,
the heart skies were blazing.
History, was about to be witnessed.
The attitude from hell, had sounded the bell,
of the attack, that was forthcoming.

Red velvet gloves, dressed the hands,
that gripped, the axe of betrayal.
The vein of recognition,
the weapons of words,
witnessed, blood being spilt,
on the streets of the heart.

Broken was the bond,
forgotten were the vows,
as love ran to the bunkers for shelter.
The black heart, had broken apart,
the safe, that held,
the treasures of tomorrow.

The streets of the heart,
were washed down, with the blood
of anger, deceit, and betrayal.
A smile stole the show,
as the calendar date read,
Today is "the twelfth of never".

## DEAR FRIEND

Fellow cosmic traveller,
as you stand so near,
if you would learn to trust me,
I could rid you of your fear.
No more tension, no more stress,
no more heartaches, no more mess,
it seems unbelievable, of that I know,
but I found the secret, "how to let go".

It's hard at first, when you do seek,
it grinds you down, it makes you meek,
they don't understand what you are all about
so to Mother Nature, you must shout.
What's going on? What's wrong with me?
And she shouts back, full of glee,
you have woken up, that is all,
take your time, "have a ball".

But waking up is hard to do,
you have to change your point of view,
what will people think and say?
Who gives a damn, in the now of this day.
Do you really need people, all that bad?
If you do, it's terribly sad,
learn to discriminate, that's the way,
do your thing, "it's Judgement Day".

When you cease to run, with the pack,
when you finally learn not, to live in lack,
your whole world, will be upside down,
the word on your lips, will be a frown.
The mystics call it the awakened state
and for you, it's not too late,
time is always on your side,
when true to yourself, "you do abide".

It is not the easiest path to follow,
a lot of hiccups, you must swallow,
no attachments to the end,
then you can truly, call me a friend.
It's a double life, but only one goal,
that is the journey to find the soul,
sometimes you will feel, like giving up,
but this is the time, "to raise your cup".

Wake up, wake up, from your dream,
view the plan, recognise the scheme,
get off this wheel of life,
end the sorrow, kill the strife.

Waking up is hard to do,
adopting a new, point of view,
shattering the illusions, covered in lace,
to find the state of "immortal grace".

## NO SEASONS IN MY HEART

There are no seasons in my heart,
when we are together, or apart,
when i am troubled, or in times of pain,
arguments are not the gain.

Seasonless is my point of view,
I hope someday, you will find it too,
in times of trouble, or when we are apart,
there are no seasons in my heart.

One dog, one bone, one splash, one stone,
in times of trouble, or times alone,
for time is endless, when spent with you,
I hope you will see, my point of view.

We've got too old, we did not stray,
now we've found, the true way,
friendship forever, was the cry of the past,
friendship in tomorrows, is guaranteed to last.

The old can only generate the new,
and in time, a new point of view,
changing our thinking, is what it's all about,
and the "I love you's" we can surely shout.

With mind games over, and attachment free,
this is surely the way to be,
the "I love you's" are not said in leisure,
but spoken of, as in "golden treasure".

Love should not be watered down,
but spoken of, as a golden crown,
a new maturity, has dawned at last,
so thank you now, to the past.

So here's to the future, here's to the past,
attachment free, guaranteed to last,
no more ripples on our love lake,
now the task is to stay awake.

Asleep in our slumber, quick to attack,
all the wrong reasons, when you look back,
seasons, and seasons, of living in lack,
was nearly the straw, that broke the love back.

So here's to our friendship, please take a bow,
here's to us living, in the "eternal now",
a new way of thinking, generates a new start,
for there are no seasons, "in my heart".

## THE STARE

Your disapproving eyes,
are glaring at me,
I am receptive,
but I do not flee.
For I am happy,
happy to be, just me,
and your disapproving eyes,
don't affect me.

Maybe the changes you need,
are being mirrored back to you.
Maybe it is time for you,
to change, your point of view.
For who is the owner of your view,
did you adopt it, in some way?
As your disapproving eyes,
turn slowly away.

# The Spiritual Fields

## Clem Stack

### *"Follow the trail series"*

This impressive book sparkles with wit, insight and uplift and one cannot fail to be enriched by this author's positive and engaging approach to life. There is a judicious balancing of practice and precept in the structuring of the text, and lively scenarios are offered as affirmations of the concepts which the author has chosen to expound.

The text is totally free from any of the tiresome pretensions one has come to associate with literature of this sort, and Clem Stack has made it his business to demystify the workings of the mind and spirit and to demonstrate that untold degrees of enlightenment, i.e. the raising of our spiritual consciousness, are within our reach if we take the time to formulate a positive way of thinking. The author's great good humour shines forth from the text to the extent that we never feel as though he is condescending or preaching from a great and superior height.

This is a friendly book, and its author has much to share. The engaging style and thoughtful presentation will ensure that this book will be of appeal to a broad cross section of readers.

### Future book titles:

The Spiritual Letters
The Spiritual Warrior

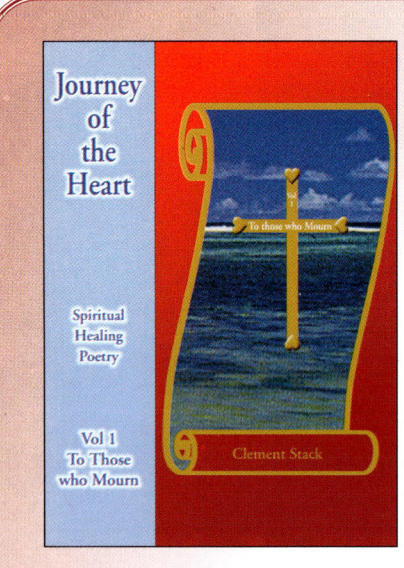

*These poems, are dedicated, to those who are experiencing, the experience of mourning. They were written, to bring comfort, and understanding, to you and your loved ones. In our age of human evolution, death is still surrounded in mysterious veils. These veils are fast, disintegrating, as we enter a new age, of understanding. Remember, we are spiritual beings, having a human experience, not human beings enjoying a spiritual experience. We come from there (home) so we must return to there.*

*Sooner or later, everybody finds themselves in a position, where they become stuck in life. regardless of the reason, the time will come, when you have to face the fact, and the daunting task, of letting go, and moving on. Courage and bravery are the fuels required for such a journey. Everything begins with the first thought, and is swiftly followed by self examination, which in its own time, will lead you to the conclusion, that you are about to become, the owner of your "brave heart",*

**Journey of the Heart Series**

**Vol. 3**     Voyage of the heart

**Vol. 4 -10**   (to follow)